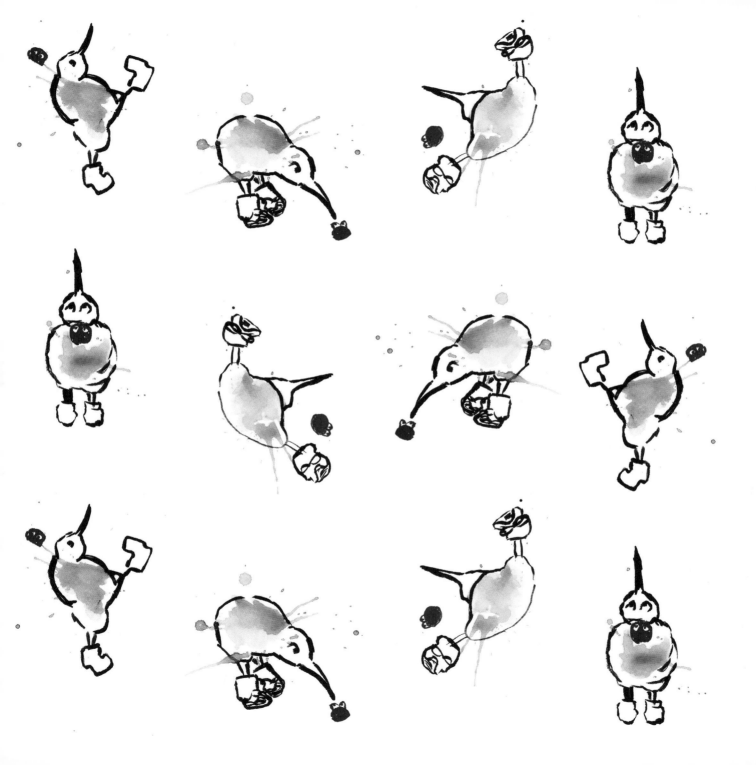

This book belongs to:

_____

_____

_____

Kiwi has always wanted to go on an adventure!

"**What is stopping me?**"
Kiwi said to herself.
So, she put her
hiking boots on
and
off she went!

"Hello Little Pebble.
Are you lost?"
asked Kiwi.

Little Pebble did not speak.
It looked **very sad**.

"You can come with me. I will **help** you find your way."

Kiwi picked up Little Pebble,

and

off they went!

On their journey, they came across lots of different paths.

"Which way do we go?"

Little Pebble did not answer...

They came across a river!

three hops!

SPLISH

SPLOSH

"Now, we have to climb this **big** hill!" said Kiwi.

Pant!

Pant!

"I am very tired,
I think you are getting
heavier
Little Pebble."

Kiwi tripped and fell into a dark cave!

Ouch!

"Are you OK Little Pebble?" asked Kiwi. Little Pebble did not answer.

"It's OK, we will get up and **keep going!**"

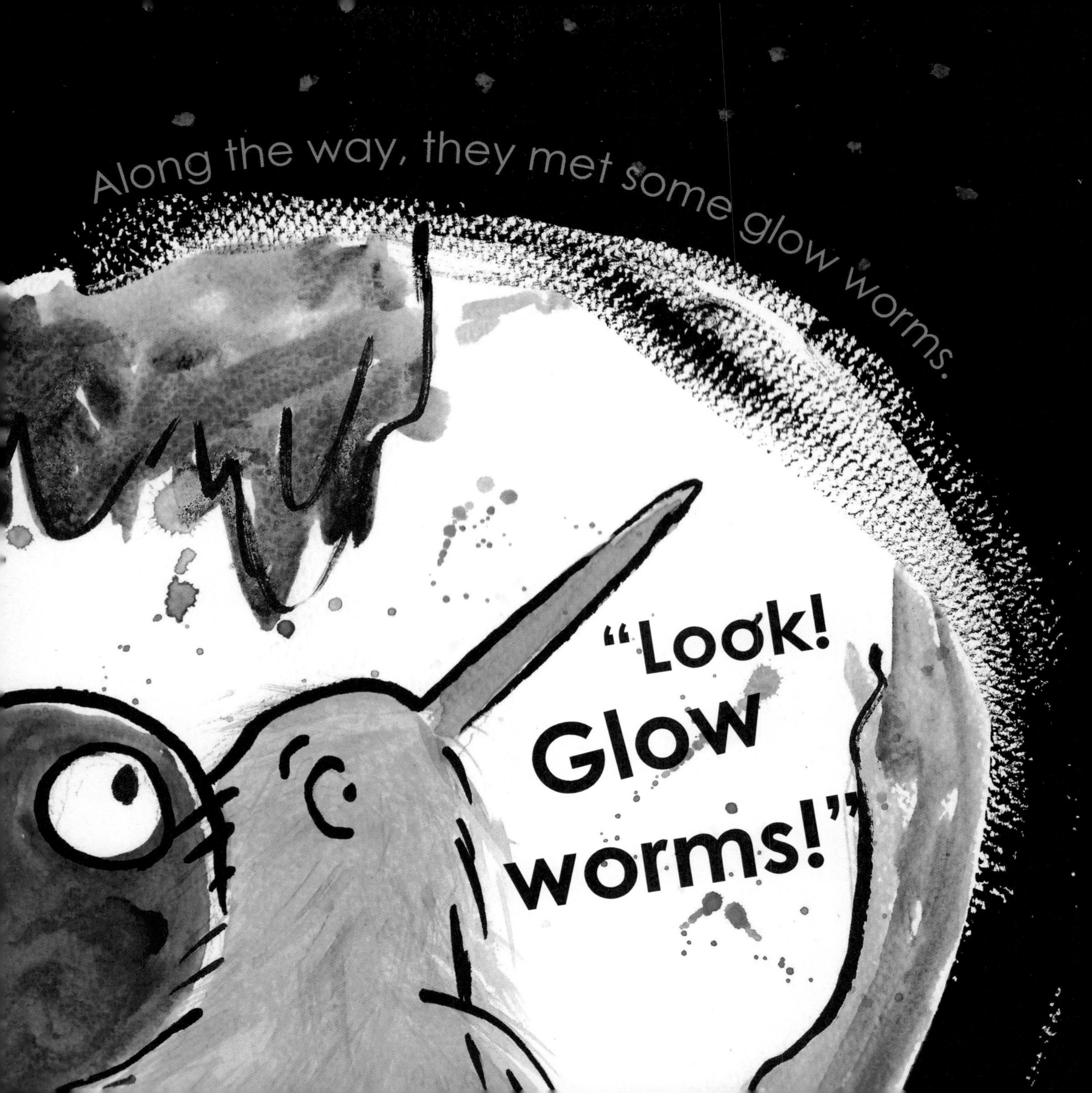

Along the way, they met some glow worms.

"Look! Glow worms!"

"Thank you, glow worms, for being so **kind.**

Even in the **darkest places,** there is still **hope."**

smiled Kiwi.

Kiwi found her
way out of the
dark cave.

She was feeling **lighter** and **happier**.
But, where did **Little Pebble go?**

Kiwi suddenly realised that
Little Pebble was
never there
this whole time.

It was how she was
feeling.

Kiwi was feeling so **sad and lost,** as though a heavy pebble was sitting on her shoulders **weighing her down.**

And as soon as she found her way, she started to find her happiness, and the heavy feeling of sadness had **disappeared.**

Now she is ready
to start her new
adventure!

"I found my path!
My path to
happiness!"
she sang.

Hello
bees!

Hello flowers!

I am Kiwi, and I am ready to explore!

Kiwi now understands,

that sometimes,

it is **OK** to feel sad.

Our pebbles come and go.
They can weigh us down,
making us feel sad and lost.

Never be afraid to ask
someone for help!

If you see a pebble
on someone else's back,
tell them you are
there to help.

You are brave
and
you are loved.

Be kind
and
dream big.

Monique Scott is an author and illustrator,
born in South Africa and lives in Northumberland
surrounded by the inspiring countryside.
She studied Illustration and Design at University of Sunderland
and has collaborated on several other books such as
Dylan's Amazing Adventures, The Elf who Saved Christmas, Fairie Forest,
Granny Green's Bedtime Stories, and Santa Ste and the Baby Dragon.
Her first written and illustrated book, 'Two Little Mice'
was released in 2018.

I would like to thank
all my family, friends and everyone
who has helped me on my creative journey,
and for seeing the pebble on my back.
Your help and support means the world to me.

Drawing is my life,
and sharing my stories is from my heart.

Never give up your dreams.

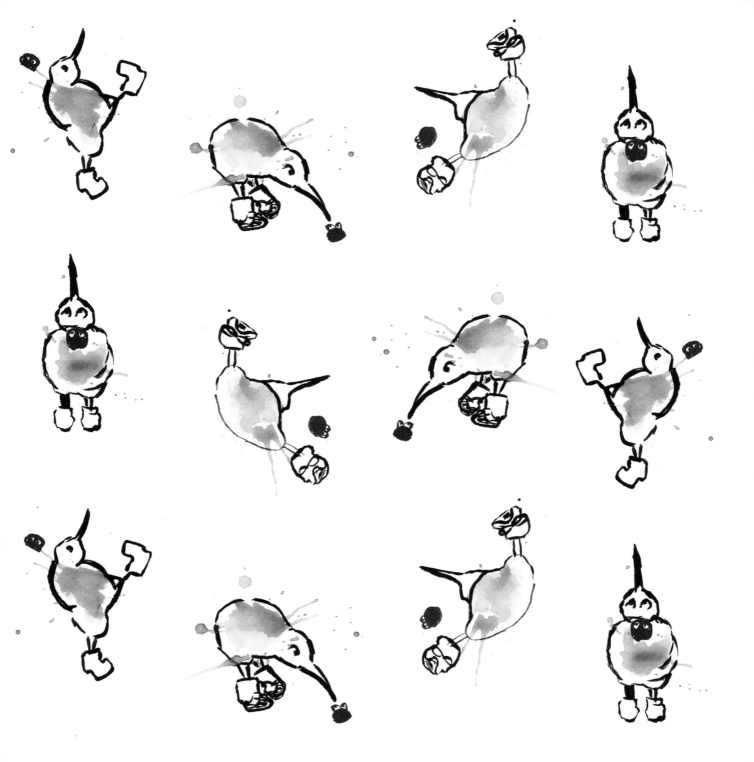

Printed in Poland
by Amazon Fulfillment
Poland Sp. z o.o., Wrocław